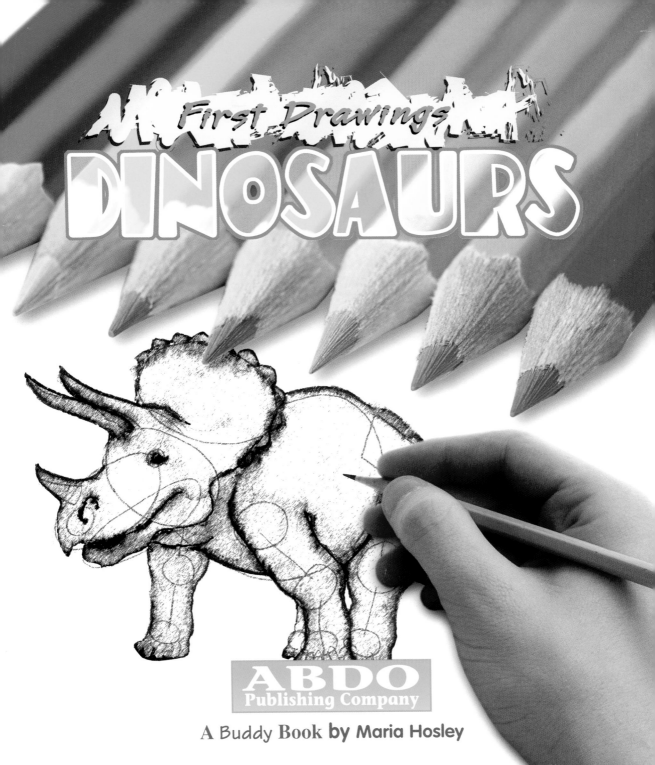

First Drawings
DINOSAURS

ABDO
Publishing Company

A Buddy Book **by Maria Hosley**

VISIT US AT
www.abdopublishing.com

Published by ABDO Publishing Company, 4940 Viking Drive, Edina, Minnesota 55435.

Copyright © 2007 by Abdo Consulting Group, Inc. International copyrights reserved in all countries. No part of this book may be reproduced in any form without written permission from the publisher. Buddy Books™ is a trademark and logo of ABDO Publishing Company.

Printed in the United States.

Editor: Sarah Tieck
Contributing Editor: Michael P. Goecke
Graphic Design: Maria Hosley
Illustrations: Maria Hosley
Interior Photographs: Banana Stock

Library of Congress Cataloging-in-Publication Data

Hosley, Maria.
    Dinosaurs / Maria Hosley.
       p. cm.
    Includes index.
    ISBN-13: 978-1-59679-802-1
    ISBN-10: 1-59679-802-5
    1. Dinosaurs in art—Juvenile literature. 2. Drawing—Technique—Juvenile literature. [1. Dinosaurs in art. 2. Drawing—Technique.] I. Title.

NC780.5.H67 2007
743.6—dc22

                         2006032539

Table Of Contents

Getting Started

Today you're going to learn to draw a dinosaur. Not sure you know how to draw? If you know how to make circles, squares, and triangles, you can draw most anything!

You will learn to draw in four steps. First, you will measure to get the correct sizes. Next, you will lightly draw the basic shapes. This helps you construct a dinosaur. From those basic shapes, you will make the final outline. And last, you will erase the basic shape lines and add **detail**.

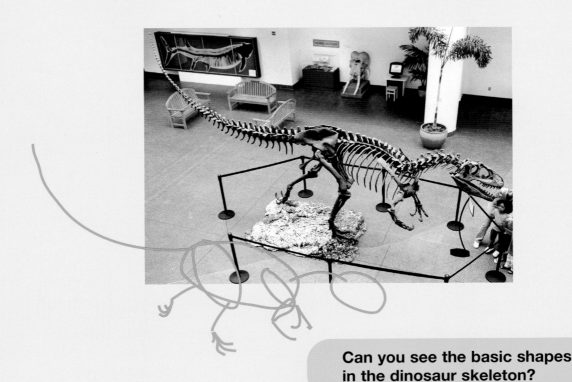

Can you see the basic shapes
in the dinosaur skeleton?

To draw a dinosaur, you'll need paper, a sharpened pencil, a big eraser, and a hard, flat surface. Many artists like to draw at a table or a desk. They sit up straight with their tools in front of them. Gather your supplies. Then, let's get started!

ARTIST'S TOOLBOX

Dinosaurs lived long before there were people. We know about them because of **fossils**. Scientists compare fossilized bones with modern animals. They use this information to learn about dinosaurs.

There are no photographs of dinosaurs. Every picture of a dinosaur was drawn by an artist. Artists use scientific information to create dinosaur drawings.

For your dinosaur drawing, you will study a **reference** picture of a dinosaur skeleton. You can also use pictures of dinosaurs to come up with your own dinosaur drawing.

Measurements and Proportions

Have you ever looked at a drawing and thought about whether it looks real? Many people draw dinosaurs that look very real.

To make a **realistic** drawing from a skeleton, begin with the dinosaur's proportions. Proportion is the size of one thing compared to another. For example, the dinosaur's head should be a size that fits with the rest of its body. Using correct proportions helps make your dinosaur drawing look realistic.

There's an easy way to match the proportions of a dinosaur skeleton to your drawing. You can use strips of paper to measure the parts in the picture. Here's how to do it:

Cut a strip of paper the same width as the dinosaur's skull. Then, make several more strips of the same size.

Lay the strips on the dinosaur. Do this to compare the head size with the width and the height of the skeleton.

The tip of the nose to the start of the tail is a little less than 4 strips.

The dinosaur's height is a little more than 2 strips.

Choosing A Size For Your Drawing

To draw this dinosaur at this size, cut several strips of paper that match the length of the orange strips shown above.

If you want a larger drawing, cut longer strips. And if you want a smaller drawing, cut shorter strips. Just make sure the strips fit on your drawing paper.

Place your cut strips on your drawing paper. Arrange them so they match the reference picture. With your pencil, lightly mark the ends of each strip.

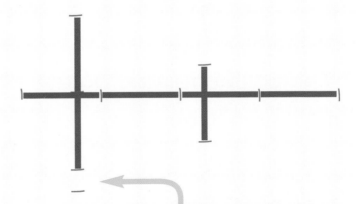

Add a little extra room here because the dinosaur is taller than 2 strips.

Basic Shapes

All things are easier to draw if you break them down into basic shapes. Draw these shapes *very lightly*. They are only a guide that you will erase later. And when the lines are light, it is easy to erase and try again. Remember to use your proportion lines as a guide!

Between the two head guidelines draw a wide, slanted oval. **Sketch** a larger oval for the body. Add ovals to form the leg parts. Last, draw lines to indicate the feet, tail, neck, and claws.

Leaving the strips on the reference picture will help you position your shapes.

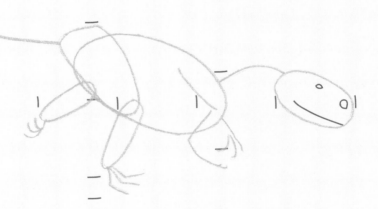

Look at the skeleton to see where the dinosaur's eyes and mouth were. Draw those lines in now to use as a guide.

Final Outline

Now you have drawn the basic shapes for your dinosaur! You can use them to make the final outline shape. Do this *lightly* with a pencil.

Follow around the outside of the basic shapes to give your dinosaur shape. Draw the legs and the tail. Add lines to shape the eyes, nose, and mouth. Last, put in lines to define the feet and the claws.

Adding Detail

Once you are happy with your outline, erase the basic shape lines. Be careful not to erase any lines you still need.

Now you can add the **details**! Add lines where the skin would overlap such as the neck, legs, and arms. Then, round and shade the eyes, nose, and mouth.

When you are happy with your outline and **details**, you can make them darker. Do this with your pencil or a marker. Erase any extra lines, and you're done!

Keep Drawing

You have now finished a drawing of a dinosaur. Good job! Use these steps next time you want to draw something.

Don't worry if drawing feels like a challenge at first. Like anything else, drawing takes practice.

Have fun with your new skills. And remember to practice, practice, practice! The more you draw the better you will become.

Want to add to your drawing? Try using a washable marker to outline your dinosaur. Then, use a wet paintbrush to pull some of the marker ink onto your dinosaur.

Use dark ink to create shadows on the dinosaur's underside. These details make your drawing look realistic.

Caricature Dinosaurs

It is fun to **exaggerate** parts of the dinosaur. This is how you make a caricature. A caricature is a picture that looks like a cartoon.

Chose one body part or feature of the dinosaur. Then, exaggerate it to make it look funny. Just use your imagination!

You can make a dinosaur have human facial **expressions**. Practice drawing dinosaur faces that show emotion. Then, try making the body position match its mood.

HAPPY

angry

scared

Using the same basic shapes, we created a caricature of the dinosaur. We tilted his head and body up and pulled his mouth together. Last, we gave motion lines to his tail and body. These details make him look like he's enjoying some music.

Important Words

detail a minor decoration, such as wrinkles in skin.

exaggerate to make something seem larger than it really is.

expression a look that shows feeling.

fossil remains of very old animals and plants commonly found in the ground. A fossil can be a bone, a footprint, or any trace of life.

realistic showing things as they are in real life.

reference a picture or an item used for information or help.

sketch to make a rough drawing.

Web Sites

To learn more about drawing dinosaurs, visit ABDO Publishing Company on the World Wide Web. Web site links about drawing dinosaurs are featured on our Book Links page. These links are routinely monitored and updated to provide the most current information available.

www.abdopublishing.com

Index